the
cocktailhour

RYLAND
PETERS
& SMALL

LONDON NEW YORK

the
cocktail hour

Ben Reed

photography by william lingwood

Senior Designer Sonya Nathoo
Editor Delphine Lawrance
Head of Production Patricia Harrington
Art Director Leslie Harrington
Publishing Director Alison Starling

Mixologist Ben Reed
Stylist Helen Trent

First published in Great Britain in 2002.
This revised edition published in 2010
by Ryland Peters & Small
20–21 Jockey's Fields
London WC1R 4BW
www.rylandpeters.com

10 9 8 7 6 5 4 3 2

Text © Ben Reed 2002, 2010
Design and photographs © Ryland Peters & Small 2002, 2010
Image p.6 © Hulton/Archive
The recipes in this book were originally published in *Cool Cocktails*
by Ben Reed.

ISBN 978 1 84975 051 6
A CIP record for this book is available from the British Library.
Printed in China.

contents

the cocktail hour

The origin of the word 'cocktail' is steeped in myth with a number of explanations for its derivation. Among my favourites is the story of the publican who, during the American War of Independence, lost one of his finest fighting cockerels. He was inconsolable until the day an army lieutenant came riding into town with the bird. The publican mixed up a special concoction and served it to the soldier, toasting him with the phrase 'to the cock's tail' (for returning the bird with all the feathers in its tail intact).

Although many cocktails we regard as 'classic' were invented before the 20th century, they came into their own in the 1900s. With palates and spirits growing more refined, cocktails were created that celebrated the base spirit rather than hid it.

Social circumstances determined how people drank. Prohibition taught Americans the joy of light, Cuban-style cocktails like the Daquiri and the Great Depression saw the emergence of the Tiki Movement in California with drinks such as the Mai Tai. Today the true classic cocktail is one that has withstood the test of time.

The preparation methods are often contentious – think of martini with the ubiquitous 'shaken' or 'stirred' argument. Invariably, and this is the joy with timeless cocktails, when a cocktail can be made in a number of ways, a new title is often bestowed upon it and a new life given!

As cocktails evolve, we should always cherish the classic, as it gives us the base to both toast the past and mix for the future.

EQUIPMENT

Any aspiring bartender should acquire a **measure (jigger)** and a **shaker**. The modern dual-measure jigger measures both 50 ml and 25 ml (a double and a single measure). The **barspoon**, with its long spiralling handle, is useful for stirring drinks and for the gentle pouring required for layered drinks. The 'wrong', flat end can be used for muddling or crushing herbs, etc. A **muddler**, a wooden pestle for mixing or crushing

equipment
and techniques

sugar cubes, limes and herbs, and a **bartender's friend** are also handy. A **mixing glass** with strainer is used for making drinks that are stirred, not shaken. Other accessories that are useful: an **ice bucket**, **ice tongs** and a **juice squeezer**.

GLASSES

The traditional **martini glass** is a familiar icon, with its open face and slim stem. The **cocktail glass** is similar to the martini glass but with a slightly rounded bowl. The **rocks** or **old-fashioned glass** is a squat, straight-sided glass. The **highball** and the **collins glasses** come in various sizes but they are all tall, slim glasses designed to keep a long drink fresh and cold. The small, sturdy **shot glass** is designed with one purpose: getting the drink from one's glass into one's mouth with minimal fuss. The **champagne flute** is perfect for keeping the sparkle in your champagne cocktails. It should be elegant and long-stemmed, with a narrow rim to enhance the delicacy of the drink.

TECHNIQUES

There are six basic ways of creating a cocktail: **building**, **blending**, **shaking**, **stirring over ice**, **layering** and **muddling**. Whichever method you are using, measure the ingredients accurately to get the balance of tastes right. The process of **building** a cocktail just requires adding the measured ingredients to the right glass, with ice, and giving it a quick stir before serving. The **blending** method involves pouring all the ingredients into a blender, adding crushed ice and flicking the switch. Using a **shaker** is the most enjoyable way to mix a cocktail, both for you and your guests. Add the ingredients to the shaker and fill it with ice. The shaking movement should be sharp but do keep your hands on both parts of the shaker or at least a finger on the cap. Drinks containing egg white, cream and juices should be shaken for slightly longer than the usual ten seconds. **Stirring** is the best method when you want to retain the clarity and strength of the spirits in cocktails such as a Manhattan. Use an ice-filled mixing glass and stir carefully to avoid chipping the ice and diluting the drink. Frost your serving glasses by leaving them in the freezer for an hour before use. **Layering** is used for drinks such as the White Russian. With the flat end of a barspoon resting on the surface of the base spirit, pour each of the remaining spirits in turn down the handle of the spoon. This keeps the ingredients separate and allows them to be tasted one at a time. **Muddling** involves using the flat end of a barspoon or a muddler to mix or crush ingredients such as fruit or herbs to gently release the flavours.

Pink Gin is a thoroughly British cocktail which deserves a premium gin. Although it originated as a medicinal potion in the British Navy, **Pink Gin** became one of the smartest drinks in 1940s' London.

pink gin

50 ml gin
a dash of Angostura bitters

Rinse a frosted sherry or martini glass with Angostura bitters, add chilled gin and serve.

classic
dry martini

50 ml gin
a dash of dry vermouth
green olive

Using a mixing glass, chill
the gin and vermouth over
ice and pour into a frosted
martini glass. Garnish
with a green olive.

The **Classic Dry Martini** has long been considered the ultimate in sophistication and elegance. Its roots date back as far as the 1840s where it is believed to have been served at a bar in Martinez, California. The **FDR** (so named after President Roosevelt) and the **Smoky Martini** are popular variations on the stylish classic.

fdr martini

ALSO KNOWN AS THE DIRTY MARTINI
50 ml gin
a dash of dry vermouth
12.5 ml olive brine
green olive

Add the gin, a dash of dry vermouth and the olive brine to a shaker filled with cracked ice. Shake sharply and strain into a frosted martini glass. Garnish with an olive.

smoky martini

50 ml gin
a dash of dry vermouth
a dash of whisky

This is a variation on the FDR Martini, with the whisky replacing the olive brine, but the method is identical.

The **Bronx** dates back to the days of Prohibition, when gang bosses reigned and booze played an important part in the economy of the underworld. Different areas of New York became known for the special cocktails they offered, such as this speciality of the Bronx district. Like the Manhattan, it has three variations: the dry, the sweet and the perfect. The **Silver** and **Golden Bronx** are variations on the perfect, with the addition of egg white or egg yolk.

silver bronx

50 ml gin
a dash of dry vermouth
a dash of sweet vermouth
50 ml fresh orange juice
1 egg white

Shake all the ingredients vigorously over ice and strain into a chilled cocktail glass.

golden bronx

The method is the same as for the silver bronx, but replace the egg white with an egg yolk.

gin gimlet

50 ml gin
25 ml lime cordial

Pour the gin and cordial into a
shaker filled with ice. Shake very
sharply and strain through a sieve
into a frosted martini glass.

Originally made for officers on British naval
vessels in the 1800s, the **Gin Gimlet** should
be shaken vigorously to ensure it is chilled to
perfection, then strained before serving to catch
any ice chips. If you are making a **Journalist**,
watch the measurements; it's a drink that
needs to be finely balanced.

the journalist

50 ml gin
10 ml sweet vermouth
10 ml dry vermouth
5 ml fresh lemon juice
5 ml triple sec
1 dash Angostura bitters

Shake all the ingredients over ice
and strain into a frosted martini glass.

Two offshoots of the original Gin Fizz, (a classic that some would say should remain untouched) these cocktails are classics in their own right. The substitution of the soda by champagne in the **Royal Gin Fizz** helps to make it special and lends it a little extra fizz. The addition of the rose flower water in the **New Orleans** or **Ramos Fizz** accentuates the juniper in the gin and the cream gives this very light drink a little more body.

royal gin fizz

50 ml gin
25 ml fresh lemon juice
1 barspoon white sugar
   (or 12.5 ml sugar syrup)
champagne
1 egg white

Put the egg white, gin, lemon juice and sugar into a shaker filled with ice and shake vigorously. Strain into a collins glass filled with ice. Top up with champagne.

new orleans fizz

ALSO KNOWN AS THE RAMOS FIZZ
50 ml gin
25 ml fresh lemon juice
1 barspoon white sugar
   (or 12.5 ml sugar syrup)
12.5 ml rose flower water
   (or orange flower water)
12.5 ml single cream
a dash of egg white
soda water

Add all the ingredients, except the soda water, to a shaker filled with ice. Shake vigorously and strain into a highball over ice. Gently add the soda water, stirring with a barspoon while doing so.

VODKA

The **Black** and **White Russians** are classics that have been on the scene since the Cold War era. They make stylish after-dinner cocktails with their sweet coffee flavour, which is sharpened up by the vodka. The White Russian, with its addition of the cream float, is even more appropriate as a nightcap.

black russian

50 ml vodka
25 ml Kahlúa coffee liqueur
stemmed cherry

Shake the vodka and Kahlúa together over ice and strain into a rocks glass filled with ice. Garnish with a stemmed cherry.

white russian

For a White Russian, layer 25 ml single cream into the glass of Black Russian over the back of a barspoon. Garnish with a stemmed cherry.

silver streak

25 ml chilled vodka
25 ml kümmel

Pour a generous single
measure of chilled vodka
into a rocks glass filled with
ice. Add a similar amount of
kümmel, stir and serve.

The first **Vodkatini** dates back to the 1940s. As with the Classic Dry Martini, there are four important things to consider when making it: the quantity of vermouth, to shake or stir, straight up or on the rocks, an olive or a twist. The **Silver Streak** calls for kümmel which has a distinctive, aniseed-like taste that comes from the caraway seeds used in its production.

vodkatini

50 ml vodka
a dash of dry vermouth
pitted olive or lemon zest

Fill a mixing glass with ice and stir with a barspoon until the glass is chilled. Tip the water out and top with ice. Add a dash of dry vermouth and continue stirring. Strain the liquid away and top with ice. Add a large measure of vodka and stir until it is chilled (take care not to chip the ice and dilute the vodka). Strain into a frosted martini glass and garnish.

harvey wallbanger

50 ml vodka
12.5 ml Galliano
fresh orange juice
orange slice

Pour a large measure of vodka into a highball glass filled with ice. Fill the glass almost to the top with orange juice and pour in a float of Galliano. Garnish with an orange slice and serve with a swizzle stick and straw.

The story goes that Harvey, a Californian surfer who had performed particularly badly in an important contest, visited his local bar to drown his sorrows. He ordered his usual screwdriver - only to decide that it wasn't strong enough for what he had in mind. Scanning the bar for something to boost his drink, his eyes fell on the distinctively shaped Galliano bottle, a shot of which was then added to his drink as a float. Needless to say, his resultant state after a few of these was so rocky that, as he searched for the door on the way out, he bounced off a couple of walls before spilling out onto the street. Harvey Wallbanger, they called him.

The **Moscow Mule** celebrates the godsend that is ginger beer. It lends the Mule its legendary kick and an easy spiciness. The **Bloody Mary** has been a renowned hangover cure or pick-me-up for years. Curing hangovers can be painless, and should be enjoyable too. They are an aspect of bartending that cannot be ignored – and, in a truly biblical way, what the bartender giveth so shall he take away.

bloody mary

50 ml vodka
200 ml tomato juice
2 grinds of black pepper
2 dashes of Worcestershire sauce
2 dashes of Tabasco sauce
2 dashes of fresh lemon juice
1 barspoon horseradish sauce
1 celery stick

Shake all the ingredients over ice and strain into a highball glass filled with ice. Garnish with a celery stick. (These measurements are dependent on personal tastes for spices.)

moscow mule

50 ml vodka
1 lime
ginger beer

Pour a large measure of vodka into a highball filled with ice. Cut the lime into quarters, squeeze and drop into the glass. Top with ginger beer and stir with a barspoon. Serve with a straw.

WHISKY

The naming of Manhattan Island comes from 'Manhachtanienck' which roughly translates as 'the island where we were intoxicated', so called by Lenape Indians after drinking a dark spirit.

For each cocktail, chill the ingredients, add to a mixing glass filled with ice and stir until further chilled. Strain into a frosted martini glass, add the garnish and serve.

dry manhattan

50 ml rye whiskey
25 ml dry vermouth
a dash of Angostura bitters
lemon zest

perfect
manhattan

50 ml rye whiskey
12.5 ml sweet vermouth
12.5 ml dry vermouth
a dash of Angostura bitters
maraschino cherry

sweet
manhattan

50 ml rye whiskey
25 ml sweet vermouth
a dash of Angostura bitters
maraschino cherry

old fashioned

50 ml bourbon
1 white sugar cube
2 dashes of orange bitters
orange zest

Place the sugar cube soaked with orange bitters
into a rocks glass, muddle the mixture with a barspoon
and add a dash of bourbon along with a couple of
ice cubes. Keep adding ice and bourbon and keep
muddling until the full 50 ml has been added to the
glass (ensuring the sugar has dissolved). Rim the
glass with a strip of orange and drop it into the glass.

The **Old Fashioned**, the **Mint Julep** and the **Rusty Nail** have one thing in common – they are all timeless whisky cocktails that never fail to delight. As those among us who are already connoisseurs of the water of life will tell you, each cocktail should be sipped and savoured.

mint julep

50 ml bourbon
2 sugar cubes
5 sprigs of mint

Crush the mint and sugar cubes in the bottom of a collins glass. Fill the glass with crushed ice and add the bourbon. Stir the mixture vigorously with a barspoon and serve.

rusty nail

30 ml whisky
30 ml Drambuie
orange zest

Add both ingredients to a glass filled with ice and muddle with a barspoon. Garnish with a zest of orange.

boston sour

50 ml bourbon
20 ml fresh lemon juice
15 ml sugar syrup
2 dashes of Angostura bitters
a dash of egg white
lemon slice and maraschino cherry

Add all the ingredients to a shaker
filled with ice and shake sharply. Strain
the contents into a whisky tumbler filled
with ice, garnish with a lemon slice and
a maraschino cherry.

Reputed to be the very first cocktail, the **Sazerac** has been around since the 1830s. To fully enjoy its flavours the Sazerac should be drunk undiluted. The classic Sour is made with Scotch, but since I like my sours a little on the sweet side I prefer the vanillary sweetness of this bourbon-based **Boston Sour**.

new orleans sazerac

50 ml bourbon
25 ml Pernod
1 sugar cube
a dash of Angostura bitters

Rinse an old fashioned glass with Pernod and discard the Pernod. Put the sugar in the glass, saturate with Angostura bitters, then add ice cubes and the bourbon then serve.

The **Hot Toddy**, with its warming blend of spices and sweet honey aroma, has long been the perfect comforter and will soothe any aches, snuffles and alcohol withdrawal symptoms that your illness may have inflicted upon you. It's also a great life-saver for cold afternoons spent outside watching sport. Next time you have need to pack a thermos flask of coffee, think again – mix up a batch of Hot Toddies, and see how much more popular you are than the next man!

hot toddy

50 ml whisky
25 ml fresh lemon juice
2 barspoons honey or sugar syrup
75 ml hot water
1 cinnamon stick
5 whole cloves
2 lemon slices

Spear the cloves into the lemon slices and add them to a heatproof glass or a toddy glass along with the rest of the ingredients.

The **Mai Tai** was originally made in the 1940s by Victor Bergeron (Trader Vic) in California. With its complex mixture of flavours it has as many variations as it has garnishes. The one thing that most bartenders seem to agree on is that a thick, dark rum should be used, along with all the fruit-based ingredients that lend the classic its legendary fruitiness.

RUM, TEQUILA & CACHAÇA

mai tai

25 ml aged Jamaican
dark rum
25 ml golden rum
30 ml lime juice
20 ml orange curaçao
10 ml orgeat syrup
10 ml sugar syrup
a mint sprig

Add all the ingredients
to a cocktail shaker filled
with ice, shake and strain
into an ice-filled glass.
Garnish with a pineapple
slice and a mint sprig.
Serve with straws.

orange daiquiri

50 ml light rum
20 ml fresh lemon juice
10 ml sugar syrup

Measure all the ingredients and pour
into an ice-filled shaker. Shake and
strain into a frosted martini glass.

original daiquiri

50 ml golden rum
25 ml fresh lime juice
3 barspoons sugar syrup

Measure all the ingredients and pour
into an ice-filled shaker. Shake and
strain into a frosted martini glass.

bacardi cocktail

50 ml Bacardi white rum
a dash of grenadine
juice of 1 small lime
1 barspoon of powdered sugar
  or a dash of sugar syrup

Shake all the ingredients
sharply over ice, then strain
into a frosted martini glass
and serve.

The **Original Daiquiri** is a classic cocktail that was made famous
at El Floridita restaurant Havana, early in the 20th century. It has as
many recipe variations as famous drinkers (Hemingway always ordered
doubles at El Floridita) but once you have found the perfect balance,
stick to those measurements exactly. The **Orange Daiquiri** and
Bacardi Cocktail are two of the best-known variations.

A sweet, creamy drink that, for a time, epitomized the kind of cocktail disapproved of by 'real' cocktail drinkers (compare a **Piña Colada** with a Classic Dry Martini!). However, since its creation in the 1950s, it has won widespread popularity. Do not feel ashamed to order this modern day kitsch classic – there is a reason it is still served in bars the world over.

piña colada

50 ml golden rum
25 ml coconut cream
12.5 ml cream
25 ml fresh pineapple juice
a slice of pineapple

Put all the ingredients into a blender, add an ice scoop of crushed ice and blend. Pour into a sour or collins glass and garnish with a slice of pineapple.

rum runner

25 ml white rum
25 ml dark rum
juice of 1 lime
15 ml sugar syrup
150 ml fresh pineapple juice

Shake all the ingredients sharply
over ice in a shaker and strain into a
highball glass filled with crushed ice.

The **Rum Runner** is a perfect example of rum's affinity with fresh juices.
Rum also has the ability to hold its own when combined with quite a selection
of other flavours. The **Planter's Punch** recipe can never be forgotten since
Myers has very kindly put the recipe on the back label of its rum bottle. A great
favourite for parties because it can be made in advance, Planter's Punch can
be prepared in an old oak barrel for authenticity but a big bowl will do, with
slices of fruit added, such as oranges, melons, apples and pears. The **T-Punch**
is a refreshing drink, perfect for a hot summer's day, and can be made according
to taste with more lime or more sugar for a quick variation on the theme.

planter's punch

50 ml Myers rum
juice of half a lemon
50 ml fresh orange juice
a dash of sugar syrup
soda water
orange slice

Pour all the ingredients, except the soda water, into a cocktail shaker filled with ice, shake and strain into a ice-filled highball. Top up with soda water and garnish with a slice of orange.

t-punch

1 lime wedge
1 heaped teaspoon
  muscovado sugar
50 ml rhum agricole

Put the sugar in the bottom of an old-fashioned glass. Squeeze the lime and drop into the glass. Pound with a muddler to break up and dissolve the sugar. Add the rum and ice, stir and serve.

The **Mojito**, with its alluring mix of mint and rum, invariably whisks its drinker away to warmer climes. Championed by Hemingway in the 1940s and wildly popular in Miami for years, this Cuban concoction can now be found gracing the menus of discerning cocktail bars worldwide.

mojito

50 ml golden rum
5 sprigs of mint
2 dashes of sugar syrup
a dash of fresh lime juice
soda water

Put the mint into a highball, add the rum, lime juice and sugar syrup and press with a barspoon until the aroma of the mint is released. Add the crushed ice and stir vigorously until the mixture and the mint is spread evenly. Top with soda water and stir again. Serve with straws.

cuba libre

50 ml white rum
1 lime
cola

Pour the rum into a highball
filled with ice; cut a lime into
eighths, squeeze and drop
the wedges into the glass.
Top with cola and serve with
straws.

One of the most famous of all rum-based drinks, the **Cuba Libre** was reputed to have been invented by an army officer in Cuba shortly after Coca Cola was first produced in the 1890s. Cachaça, a spirit indigenous to Brazil is distilled directly from the juice of sugar cane, unlike white rum, which is usually distilled from molasses. The **Caipirinha** has made cachaça popular in many countries.

caipirinha

50 ml cachaça
1 lime
2 brown sugar cubes

Cut the lime into eighths, squeeze and place into an old-fashioned glass with the sugar cubes, then pound well with a pestle. Fill the glass with crushed ice and add the cachaça. Stir vigorously and serve with a straw.

tequila slammer

50 ml gold tequila
50 ml champagne
(chilled)

Pour both the
tequila and the
chilled champagne
into a small collins
glass with a sturdy
base. Hold a napkin
over the glass
(sealing the liquid
inside), sharply
slam the glass
down onto a stable
surface and drink in
one go while it is
still fizzing.

margarita

50 ml gold tequila
20 ml triple sec
(or Cointreau)
20 ml lime juice

Shake all the
ingredients sharply
with cracked ice.
Strain into a chilled
cocktail glass
rimmed with salt.

The **Margarita** is the cocktail most closely
associated with tequila. This is the classic
recipe, but when you are making it at home
there is no right or wrong way – just your
way! You can use Cointreau or Grand Marnier
or indeed any orange-flavoured liqueur but
only add lime juice and never, ever use a
ready-made premix. The **Tequila Slammer**
is a drink that needs to be handled with care.
This one is more likely to be imbibed for the
sensation rather than the taste!

BRANDY, LIQUEURS & APERITIFS

brandy alexander

50 ml brandy
12.5 ml crème de cacao
   (dark and white)
12.5 ml double cream
nutmeg

Shake all the ingredients over ice
and strain into a frosted martini glass.
Garnish with a sprinkle of nutmeg.

The **Brandy Alexander** is the perfect
after-dinner cocktail, luscious and seductive
and great for chocolate lovers. It's important,
though, to get the proportions right so that
the brandy stands out as the major investor.

The **Stinger** is a great palate cleanser and digestif and, like brandy, should be consumed after dinner. The amount of crème de menthe added depends on personal taste. The **Sidecar**, like many of the classic cocktails created in the 1920s, is attributed to the inventive genius of Harry MacElhone, who founded Harry's New York Bar in Paris. It is said to have been created in honour of an eccentric military man who would roll up outside the bar in the sidecar of his chauffeur-driven motorcycle. It is certainly the cocktail choice of people who know precisely what they want.

stinger

50 ml brandy
25 ml crème de menthe (white)

Shake the ingredients together over ice and strain into a frosted martini glass.

sidecar

50 ml brandy
juice of half a lemon
12.5 ml Cointreau

Shake all the ingredients
together over ice and
strain into a frosted
martini glass with a
sugared rim.

americano

25 ml Campari
25 ml sweet vermouth
soda water
1 orange slice

Build the ingredients over ice
into a highball glass, stir and
serve with an orange slice.

The **Americano** and the **Negroni** have, of course, been around for a long time. The Americano is a refreshing blend of bitter and sweet, topped with soda to make the perfect thirst quencher for a hot summer afternoon. The Negroni packs a powerful punch but still makes an elegant aperitif. For a drier variation, add a little more dry gin, but if a fruitier cocktail is more to your taste, wipe some orange zest around the top of the glass and add some to the drink.

negroni

25 ml Campari
25 ml sweet vermouth
25 ml gin
orange zest

Build all the ingredients into a rocks glass filled with ice, garnish with a twist of orange zest and stir well. For an extra-dry Negroni, add a little more gin.

The **Golden Cadillac** is not a drink to be approached lightly, and you could be excused for raising your eyebrows at the possibility of mixing crème de cacao (chocolate flavoured) with orange juice and Galliano (herb and liquorice flavoured). If the thought of this combination is too much for you, try substituting the crème de cacao with Cointreau to create another popular cocktail called Golden Dream. The **Grasshopper** is a more obvious combination of peppermint and cream, the perfect drink for after dinner.

golden cadillac

25 ml crème de cacao (white)
25 ml single cream
50 ml fresh orange juice
a dash of Galliano

Shake all the ingredients over ice, strain into a frosted martini glass and serve.

grasshopper

25 ml crème de menthe (white)
12.5 ml crème de menthe (green)
25 ml single cream

Shake all the ingredients over ice, strain into a frosted martini glass and serve.

CHAMPAGNE

25 ml brandy
1 white sugar cube
2 dashes of Angostura bitters
dry champagne

Moisten the sugar cube
with Angostura bitters
and place in a champagne
flute. Add the brandy,
then gently pour in the
champagne and serve.

champagne cocktail

This cocktail has truly stood the test of time, as popular now as when it was sipped by the stars of the silver screen in the 1940s. It's a simple and delicious cocktail that epitomizes the elegance and sophistication of that era and still lends that same touch of urbanity to those who drink it nowadays.

If there is another drink in the world that looks more tempting and drinkable than a **Black Velvet**, then please, someone make it for me now. Pour this drink gently into the glass to allow for the somewhat unpredictable nature of both the Guinness and the champagne. The **Bellini** originated in Harry's Bar in Venice in the early 1940s and became a favourite of the movers and shakers of chic society. Although there are many variations on this recipe, there is one golden rule for the perfect Bellini – always use fresh, ripe peaches to make the peach juice.

black velvet

Guinness
champagne

Half fill a champagne
flute with Guinness,
top with champagne
and serve.

bellini

¼ fresh peach,
skinned
12.5 ml crème de
pèche
a dash of peach
  bitters (optional)
champagne
peach ball

Blend the peach
and add to a flute.
Pour in the crème
de pèche and the
peach bitters, if
using, and top up
with champagne,
stirring carefully
and continuously.
Garnish with a
peach ball in the
bottom of the glass,
then serve.

james bond

25 ml vodka
1 white sugar cube
2 dashes of Angostura bitters
champagne

Moisten the sugar cube
with Angostura bitters and
put into a martini glass.
Cover the sugar cube with
the vodka and gently top
with champagne.

french 75

50 ml gin
25 ml fresh lemon juice
12.5 ml sugar syrup
champagne
lemon zest

Shake the gin, lemon juice and sugar
syrup over ice and strain into a flute. Top
with champagne and garnish with a long
strip of lemon zest.

The **James Bond** is a variation on the
Champagne Cocktail, using vodka instead
of the more traditional brandy. The naming
of this cocktail is a mystery to me since the
eponymous spy liked his drinks shaken! The
French 75 is another classic cocktail from
Harry's New York Bar in Paris. It's not
dissimilar to a Gin Sling, but is topped
up with champagne instead of soda water.

index